To My Son

with Love

ISBN: 978-1-68088-074-8

◫ and Blue Mountain Press are registered in U.S. Patent and Trademark Office.
Certain trademarks are used under license.

Printed in China.
First Printing: 2016

♽ This book is printed on recycled paper.

This book is printed on paper that has been specially produced to be acid free
(neutral pH) and contains no groundwood or unbleached pulp. It conforms with the
requirements of the American National Standards Institute, Inc., so as to ensure that
this book will last and be enjoyed by future generations.

Blue Mountain Arts, Inc.
P.O. Box 4549, Boulder, Colorado 80306

To My Son
with Love

Susan Polis Schutz

Illustrated by
Stephen Schutz

Blue Mountain Press™
Boulder, Colorado

To My Son
with Love

To see you happy —
laughing and joking
smiling and content
striving toward goals of your own
accomplishing what you set out to do
having fun
capable of loving and being loved
is what I always wished for you

Today I thought about your
        handsome face
and felt your excitement for life
and your genuine happiness
and I burst with pride
as I realized that my dreams
        for you have come true
What an extraordinary person
        you have become
and as you continue to grow
please remember always
how very much
I love you

I Enjoy You So Much, My Son

I feel so fortunate to have you for a son
I love your bright face
when we talk seriously about the world
I love your enthusiasm
when you laugh at the inconsistencies
    in the world

I love your eyes
when you are showing emotion
I love your mind
when you are discovering new ideas
and creating dreams
Many people tell me that
they cannot talk to their children
that they cannot wait for them
    to leave home
I want you to know
that I enjoy you so much and
I look forward to any time we can
    spend together

I Hope You Always
Live Life to the Fullest

*D*reams can come true if you take the time to
think about what you want in life...
Get to know yourself
Find out who you are
Choose your goals carefully
Be honest with yourself
Find many interests and pursue them
Find out what is important to you
Find out what you are good at
Don't be afraid to make mistakes
Work hard to achieve successes
When things are not going right
don't give up — just try harder
Find courage inside of you to remain strong
Give yourself freedom to try out new things
Don't be so set in your ways that you can't grow
Always act in an ethical way

Laugh and have a good time
Form relationships with people you respect
Treat others as you want them to treat you
Be honest with people
Accept the truth
Speak the truth
Open yourself up to love
Don't be afraid to love
Remain close to your family
Take part in the beauty of nature
Be appreciative of all that you have
Help those less fortunate than you
Try to make other lives happy
Work toward peace in the world
Live life to the fullest

You Have Always Been Such a Gift to Me

From the day you
were born
you were
so special
so smart
so sensitive
so good
It was so much fun
to watch you

As you grew
you became your
own person
with your own ideas
with your own way
of doing things
It was so exciting
to watch you

As you grew more
you became more independent
still special
still smart
still sensitive
still good

I am so proud
of everything about you
and I want you to know
that I love
everything about you

I Remember When
You Were a Little Boy

You cared so much
about every living thing
You were so sensitive
You are older now
but you are still
the same sensitive little boy
Your eyes still radiate all the
joy and goodness in your heart
and your actions are so kind

I hope that you always keep
your wonderful attitude
that whatever happens
in your life
happens for the best
I hope that you are always
truly thankful
for whatever you have
and that you never care
about what you do not have
You are a very rare person
and I am so honored
to have you as my son
You cannot imagine
how happy you make me
I do not have to worry
about you at all
You are everything
a parent could wish for

I Am So Proud of You

You are growing up to be
an incredible young man
You are unique and special
and I know that
your talents will give you
many paths to choose from
in the future
Always keep your many interests —
they will allow your mind
to remain energized
Always keep your positive outlook —
it will give you the strength to
accomplish great things
Always keep your determination —
it will give you the ability
to succeed in meeting your goals
Always keep your excitement
about whatever you do —
it will help you to have fun
Always keep your sense of humor —
it will allow you to
make mistakes and learn from them

Always keep your confidence —
it will allow you to take risks
and not be afraid of failure
Always keep your sensitivity —
it will help you to understand
and do something about
injustices in the world
As you continue through life
in your own unique, wonderful way
always remember that
I am more proud of you
than ever before

A Son Is...

A kite flying through the trees
a tadpole turning into a frog
a dandelion in the wind
a mischievous smile
laughing eyes
a scrape on the knee
a wonder
an excitement, a burst of energy
an animation
a spirited breeze

A son is love
and everything beautiful

I Hope You'll Always Remember These Words...

$\mathcal{A}$ mother tries to provide her son
with insight into the important things in life
in order to make his life
as happy and fulfilling as possible

A mother tries to teach her son
to be kind and generous toward other people
to be honest and forthright at all times
to be fair and gentle —
treating men and women equally
to respect and learn from older people
to know himself well
to understand his strong and weak points
to accept criticism and learn from his mistakes
to have many interests to pursue
to have many goals to follow
to work hard to reach these goals

A mother tries to teach her son
to have a strong set of values and beliefs
which he will always live by
and not be afraid to defend
to listen to his intelligence
to laugh and enjoy life
to appreciate the beauty of nature...

(continued)

A mother tries to teach her son
to express his feelings openly and honestly
    at all times
to realize that love is the best emotion
    that anyone can have
to value the family unit as the basis of stability

If I have provided you with an insight
into most of these things
then I have succeeded as a mother
in what I hoped to accomplish in raising you
If many of these things slipped by
while we were all so busy
I have a feeling that you know them anyway
However, I know I have emphasized to you
to be yourself at all times
to be proud and confident
to appreciate the value of love
I have loved you so deeply at all times
I have supported you at all times
And I will always continue to love and support
everything you are and everything you do

Family Is So Important

The love
of a family
is so
uplifting

The warmth
of a family
is so
comforting

The support
of a family
is so reassuring

The attitude
of a family
toward
each other
molds one's
attitude forever
toward the
world

I Hope You'll Think of Me When You Need Someone to Talk To

Sometimes we do not feel
like we want to feel
Sometimes we do not achieve
what we want to achieve
Sometimes things happen
that do not make sense
Sometimes life leads us in directions
that are beyond our control
It is at these times most of all
that we need someone
who will quietly understand us
and be there to support us

I want you to know
that I am here for you
in every way
and remember that though
things may be difficult now
tomorrow is a new day

You Are Strong Enough to Do Anything

*Y*ou are strong enough
to counter any problems that occur —
naysayers who tell you that you can't
disappointments that leave you frustrated
stinging words of others that hurt
    your feelings
obstacles in your path that make you
    want to quit
relationships that are sad or unhealthy

And you are strong enough
to enjoy the beautiful aspects of life —
people who encourage you
friends who really care about you
kind and complimentary words of others
highlights on your individual path
    that are exciting
relationships that are worthwhile and deep
literature, music and art
solitude and nature
and your own
independence and joy

I Will Always Care About You and Your Happiness

I want you to have a life of happiness
In order for you to have this
you must have many interests
and pursue them
You must have many goals
and work toward them
You must like your work
and always try to get better

You must consider yourself a success
by being proud of doing your best
You must have fun
You must listen to your own voice
You must have peace
and not always expect perfection
You must have respect
for yourself and others
My son, when I look at you
I can see you are on the right path

I Know That Your Dreams Will Come True

*Y*ou are a unique person
and only you can do whatever
it takes to follow your dreams

So let your spirit lead you
on a path of excitement
and fulfillment
And know that
because you are a
determined, hardworking
talented and independent thinker
your dreams can
become realities

Where Did the Time Go?

It seems like just
a little while ago
you raised your tiny head
and smiled at me for the first time
and I smiled back with tears
I loved you so much then
Though you are older now
living your dreams
pursuing your own goals
I still look at your beautiful smile
to know that things are all right with you

As you keep growing and learning
striving and searching
it is very important
that you pursue your own interests
without anything holding you back
It will take time
to fully understand yourself
and to discover what you
want out of life
I know that the steps in your journey
will take you on the right path
Whatever happens in the future
I will always be cheering
for your happiness and success

I Love You More Every Day

When you were a child
you were fun to play with
But now that you are older
I can do so many more
things with you

We can talk about world events
We can discuss life in general
We can make plans
We can read the same books
We can see the same movies
We can play sports with each other
Since we like the same things
we can enjoy so much together
I never thought that I could
     love you more
than I did when you were little
But now that you are older
I have found
that I love you even more

I Have So Many Wishes for You

I wish for you to have
people to love
people in your life
who will care about you
    as much as I do
blue skies and clear days
exciting things to do

I wish for you to have
easy solutions to any problems
knowledge to make the right decisions
strength in your values
laughter and fun
goals to pursue
happiness in all that you do

I wish for you to have
beautiful experiences
each new day
as you follow
your dreams

I Love You Forever, My Wonderful Son

I am so happy
with the direction
that your life
is taking you
Your decisions and actions
are noble and intelligent
I often think about
how you were the same way
when you were a little boy
I hope that you remain strong
and in control
of your life forever

As you try out new things
and take new paths
while creating a life you want to lead
please remember that
I am always behind you
in everything you do
proud and happy
and full of love for you

About the Author and Artist

Susan Polis Schutz is an accomplished writer, poet, and documentary filmmaker. She is the author of many best-selling books of poetry illustrated by her husband, Stephen Schutz, including *To My Daughter with Love on the Important Things in Life*, which has sold over 1.8 million copies, and *To My Son with Love*, which has sold over 530,000 copies. Susan's latest undertaking is creating documentary films that make a difference in people's lives with her production company, IronZeal Films. Her films have been shown on PBS stations throughout the country and include *The Misunderstood Epidemic: Depression*, which seeks to bring greater attention to this debilitating illness; *Over 90 and Loving It*, which features people in their 90s and 100s who are living extraordinary and passionate lives; and *Anyone and Everyone*, which features a diverse group of parents and their gay children discussing their experiences. Her newest film, *It's "Just" Anxiety*, provides a very honest and insightful look at the various forms of anxiety and the ways people have tried to overcome their anxiety.

Stephen Schutz has a PhD in Physics from Princeton University and is an accomplished artist. In addition to designing and illustrating all of Susan's books, he is the genius behind bluemountain.com — the Internet greeting card service he created and cofounded with the help of his and Susan's elder son, Jared. He is also the founder of Starfall.com, an interactive website where children have fun while learning to read. In 2015, the Polis-Schutz family donated Starfall to the Starfall Education Foundation after supporting the project as a social enterprise for fifteen years.

Together, Susan and Stephen are the cofounders of Blue Mountain Arts, a popular publisher known for its distinctive greeting cards, gifts, and poetry books. Susan's poems and Stephen's artwork have been published on over 435 million greeting cards worldwide.